MILES PRESS

Indiana University South Bend Department of English

DECOHER-
ENCE

42 Miles Press
Editor, David Dodd Lee

ISBN 978-0-9830747-9-3 (pbk. alk. paper)

For permission, required to reprint or broadcast more than several lines, write to:
42 Miles Press, Department of English, Indiana University South Bend
1700 Mishawaka Avenue, South Bend, IN 46615

http://42miles.wordpress.com

Art Direction: Nicholas Kuder, Design: Logan Sheehan, Production: Paul Sizer
The Design Center, Frostic School Of Art, Western Michigan University.
Printing: McNaughton & Gunn, Inc.

DECOHERENCE

POEMS BY NATE PRITTS

ALSO BY NATE PRITTS

Post Human

Right Now More Than Ever

Sweet Nothing

Big Bright Sun

The Wonderfull Yeare

Honorary Astronaut

Sensational Spectacular

CONTENTS

A Responding Noise   7

Something Beautiful   9

Sonnet No. 44   11

Genesis Cascade   12

Beverley Road Station   13

Interference Terms   14

DECOHERENCE suite // 1   17

No Memorial   31

Snow   33

Winter Calendar   34

Rhythmic Apperception   35

Another New World   37

Action / Inaction   38

DECOHERENCE suite // 2   41

Messenger Particle   50

Landscape & Figure Composition   51

Different Deer   52

The Difficult Fruit   53

Having Consistent Expectations   54

Simultaneous Events   55

DECOHERENCE suite // 3   57

Combined Input Signal   65

Twilight   66

Watch the Ground Darken   67

Solar Collapse   68

Nothing I Hear   69

The Difficult Fruit   70

DECOHERENCE suite // 4   73

The Friend   83

A person is time not
        Speed

Lyn Hejinian   The Cell (June 11 88)

A RESPONDING NOISE

I start the day flipping between
            two open Word documents
because I don't know where
to put the words I'm thinking.
                        I drink an espresso

& feel instantly more
                more alive

more in love.
This world is so tender
                            but still so dark.
        Maybe I'm the only one left

who can't see images on my cell phone.
Everything there looks so small.
All I know is   I received something.

                I received something
& should follow that with an emotion
            of some kind   a responding noise.
I restate my position in an email
                too many times
but I learn something about myself
typing this same explanation
            over & over.
I've learned not to trust
what I'm writing   if my fingers
move too fast   on the keys.
Even just a few lines without
a pause   & it's clear that I've rushed
over some feeling or point
that is worth   my calm

      & considered real attention.
            I drive to the park
& sit on a picnic table
      try to forget about everything
except the sky between long branches
or the way the sun & clouds
            create waves.
Everything, it seems, is just waves of light.

SOMETHING BEAUTIFUL

It's warm enough to open the windows
          all of them   & stop worrying
about how much money I owe

or that I can't ever do enough to justify each breath.
But I keep going
          living under immense amounts of sky

in a world where we've stopped noticing
the clouds. We walk right over the grass
& don't ever feel sorry

                              & we can't notice everything
enough to really show our love.
I fold the laundry &   can't tell the fresh of the air

apart from the scent of the house apart
          from myself. I sit on the bed
looking out the window   & it is a pleasure

          to remember breakfast   remember
so many things it doesn't hurt to remember.
          I know that the only gift we can give to someone else

is context for all this light.
                    A graceful pair of hands shapes
          memories out of the dust

but can only make what it knows how to make
          only the thing it has the pieces for.
I move back & forth   from the living room

       up & down the stairs
out to the garage   & back in again
following something.

SONNET No. 44

The world outside isn't as damaged
as anyone expected & people
seem disappointed that life
is safe again. They wanted it to be epic
since just going to the grocery
makes us feel too normal.
At least with all this rain
one can appreciate a new color scheme.
The trees are calm & dull
in their substance. Each plop of rain
is injurious to each nimble leaf.
Green is still green even when
the atoms don't refract the same
or there is such different light. Jenny,
what do you think about this
tradition of the poet writing to the muse?
What about people always wishing
for the worst so that they have
something to talk about? Take me, for example:
I can be sitting here in a current,
these relaxed circumstances &, pow!,
my mind settles on the farthest earth
remov'd from me. My thoughts are lingering
some other where. Like Brooklyn
or Asheville or Lafayette
while obviously drenched in my now
& it kills me to be so out of whack.
Jenny, maybe there is such a thing as intrinsic
qualities. Am I a good person, meant for a good life?
Describe the place where you are
& what makes it a refuge in your thoughts.
Is that feeling transferable?
I am having a hard time getting the tone
right in this poem. Maybe it's okay
to have different feelings all at once.
You wake up blinking the ghost of strong light.

GENESIS CASCADE

The internet helps me meditate
because it is a field
upon which nothing happens

       a blank.

My head is emptied of intention
which is to say
           I am happy
to forget it is Trash Night.
Outside it is so cold
I would gladly leave this body behind.

The air is purple & the motion sensor
above the garage recognizes
      my human movement
& activates   which means

I have not yet been successful
at non-being.   I drag one bulky can
to the curb.   I kick the blue bin
that holds the recycling

& it skids down the iced driveway.
I want to sit down
     & watch the passing cars
for hours   the whole rest of the night

every star blinking out   on purpose
     gone.

BEVERLEY ROAD STATION

It's good to be skeptical in this our Modern Age

skeptical about
        the authentic nature of all the experiences around us.

Every time I'm waiting for you to come home outside Beverley Station
        sometimes calmly on the street
                        while the trains move underneath me
or freezing in my gloves & hat
                        the cold in my beard
        writing your name in the snow
all I think about is the air
        in proximity & how there will be a point

as the train approaches   that everything I hear
        you hear.

INTERFERENCE TERMS

A disruption over the calm snow
is generated in my head / the air
        a subjective reality I am being composed in
behind a window in my chair at a remove
        from the real

& is also generated by the tiny fractures in gloomy white
        this vestige of pristine / unbroken

that is now pocked with a variety of February rain
        you only see if you look the right way
though it is always there.

It's been a long cold winter   & I have forgotten myself
                on purpose
only to remember.
It's hard to do anything

when ice hardens the gears.
I used to think this clear freeze was the barren right thing
                        against which my thoughts
played out   but I realize now it is not.
When she looked through the windshield / she said
        something beautiful to me
                about a name for that type of quiet
                        that has always been denied to me
                        or that I denied myself through this
buzz of an angry & unhappy mind
                the start
        of all this trouble in winter.

DECOHERENCE
suite // 1

She said   *Remember me.*
She was asking an impossible thing.

        The complex architecture of any moment in memory.

This is what we call control
            a compression of each twinkling instant. For example

the wasp trapped between two glass panes.
            It is there now & is there forever / it is late summer / forever.

Each of several trees mingled / leaves
twisted & not caring which trunk they trace back to

            whether it is afternoon or morning.
Even right now
                I'm breathing the purest air.

Morning   one side of the sky feels open
            the other crowded with clouds
growing sullen dark or fading into light.

I should collect phrases   words & some brief context
          since so much of the discipline of my thinking
revolves around an   improvisational sense
                                        of life & how to get it written.

Then to joyfully / force all those moments
                        together!

                Sometimes we are confronted
with a map but the perspective is wrong
          & still you rush   the icy streets
from one part of town to the other
                                        the air
cold in your hair   to remind you that you're living
foolishly / in a world you can't / retreat from
          & which is under no obligation to cohere.

Each person is an irregular bundle
          of mechanisms while time
keeps moving / unsteadily & all this empty talk
                              just circles.

We are matched up according to mutual / agreement
          to discover together
                    all based on very little logic
                         but big heart.
When we talked about our memories
          it was the process & not / the disparate elements we sought
                              to examine in harmony.

We are designed
          for the moment.

No wonder I am so frantic   for now   each moment
illegible in my early morning scrawl
          latched tight as it ends so that it cannot be
scrutinized with any hope
                    of a new surge.

This progress of happening buries it
in resident tension that never stopped
          & can't ever be / gone again.

Despite any beauty
           of the composed scene

             the two of us standing together
             in the aura of each other's particles
             on an actual pier with the calm occurrence of water
             in proximity

          something is not / exact enough
for the elements to provide
salvation.

                You cannot fight against the truth
of what has happened.
                     You cannot expect metaphor
                                to comfort you

or hypothetical constructs
                            to help you see

your way to a better / soothing reality.

To create a memory worth saving / a glimmer
          on real skin.

We cannot be safe with our love nor avoid the difficulty of living.

All we note here
             is the dumb & empty attempt to control
                  those sensual fragments

willing them into something lasting
          to supplant all / impermanence

these things happening & then lost outside our sphere.

This succession is the only song
                    that gives any truth   to my experience.

                    I know there was some other living before this.
            I wished it alive in early morning
                        breathing

the birds let rain hit their feathers

& though I ache for   a moment of transcendence
I'm pretty sure I wouldn't recognize anything
other than my own self   furiously
                        at work
& refusing to look out.
I hope   sincerely
          that someone else will tell me the words

to use for my own experience   so that then
I will turn from their voice & never
          let someone force my thoughts into any shape again.

Because then I would know what I was holding.
Because I know myself best
                        in conflict.
Outside
      wind causes chaos / in the branches I can't see.

How beautifully the world falls

                                        asleep

            in the silence / each snowflake

a calm yet emblazoned reminder
            of something that is miles beyond me

& is not what I am writing here.
You put your coat on the hanger where your coat goes
            & you take your clothes from the drawer
                        now / where your clothes go now.

These coordinates have no bearing on the distances
            felt in your heart
& the pile of this / accumulation   these chilly bodies
            we keep moving through.

The surrounding buildings caught every type of sunlight
        & you said this was now a field

                against which / we could / truly see

& there was such loving detail
        in the structure of the skyline
                though my mechanical mind translated

this one gone moment

        into a construction of blunt & faded syntax
                so that this blue sky was not raging
with rare beauty

        but simply was   inexorable
                unyielding.

        Natural elements
                are fraught when seen in conflict / disharmony
with something not itself

& you told me you loved me
                        my constituent fragments
                unified only in the sunlight
as it faded in the brown of your hair.

I worry that you can only know me through talking
& that talking is imperfect.

     The speaker combines a sense of joy
in description of the world
with the reality of these inducements
       as filtered by / processed through

          a brain full of language
that so often gets it wrong.

This loose & barely correspondent glare
        the light of circumstances / the intrinsic me

or the personal identity brought to bear
           on these flickering instances of time:

this doesn't reconcile with what I tell people

                the subject only ever an ostensible one
                that everything radiates
          & builds through a network
of associations   that is created & acted upon
          in the process.

If I raise my head the right way
             I can see a mountain crest
      dark as time & folded into itself

over the incessant clamor
        of anything else too close & obstructive.

This is an image from the past / of before this current.

       You showed me a painting you were making
of a real grouping of objects.   I saw the objects

    (fruit   vase   a blue pencil   all temporarily coherent)

& the painting / in progress.
               Then later
       I opened a package from you
& it was the painting   / stopped   complete in itself

    any actual reference lost but now charged
            with the form of this
though we were gone from each other.

Sometimes the last clause is / interrupted
& absent
                    since the ambiguity of meaning is subjective anyway.

It is to me a moving target almost every time
          as in / how reliably can I say any one thing
                    & be certain of that memory / perception

as untouched by love & feeling & internal thought.
I am walking up & down the aisles of vegetables at the grocery
          & needing only anything to make dinner with.

I held your hand with faith / nothing else
          was essential though it was winter & all this normal quiet

was burying me. The number of unarticulated
          fears was growing loud / the cold sunlight of an early afternoon.

[...] we die, my Friend,
Nor we alone, but that which each man loved
And prized in his peculiar nook of earth
Dies with him, or is changed; and very soon
Even of the good is no memorial left.

William Wordsworth   "The Ruined Cottage"

NO MEMORIAL

Number up the times any one person
                        being a single person / & also a vast wired amalgam
                                of self linked to all previous iterations
stood there both wrecked & triumphant

                                        with how many
                        variations of identity
all sprawled out in infinite surrender   in forgiveness asked for
                                                                from grief

& myriad mistakes & hollow emptiness.

This number is heavy grave / inclusive of a record of regret

immutable   intractable   but also
this same body of person is known to spring joyous
                in celebration when surrounded
by friends / & again glances that best formation
                        & reaches out
                                                                please

                                        please
please remind me about that day
                        when you mentioned the light
& how it made me look like it did.
It gave me such hope / was the only
best possible solution.
                                For long minutes
I've tried to read as much as I possibly
could in an effort to submerge this.

        It's 3 pm & severe in the dignity of rain.
More minds at work   & more
participation is needed for the organization
to sing / to ever make sense.   Many more forces
                & several more possible solutions
are needed for the sun to break through
& shine all the time   against

this destroyer of grey cloud
                              drilling into my chest
with equal measures of American fear   & love
                          & impossible dreams
of how entitled we are to something beyond
simple words   to recite the being of it / pinning me
to myself & my expectations of sky
                                & all this air   this space
the light no one remembers / very well / since it is something
                    lost   to each of us   a little more
in each of the hours we live
                            with heads bowed down
/ internal acquiescence to huge anxiety / resident &
            ever increasing / in the moments when even

writing this down assuages nothing but the dying
            of each moment that rolls from me
fully realized against a field of unwritten smiles

& I can't breathe deep enough to clear my head.

I will not ever answer to anyone
            about why something isn't where it should be in my heart.

Today, we are all moving on with our lives.

SNOW

It gets hard to see when I turn off the light
but I do it anyway because I want something natural

& everything suddenly looks like itself

blue & slow. I tell Jenny
I love when the big wet flakes cover the branches.

It seems less embarrassing.

I've become obsessed with recovering distant facts
to construct new memories. So tell me

about my life   in that way when you stand outside
& look up   & the snow clouds everything.

I move the car twice
to avoid being plowed in & watch YouTube videos

of people playing video games
from start to finish
                    making every right move

& never dying. Later I will turn to a blank page
to make notes for a program I am writing
                    in human language

because it's all I know

even though it has no effect on the old technology
& it is not compatible with the newest iterations.

It's all I know
& yet it will fail.   I can't break things

into separate parts anymore.
I would like to turn fully away from one system
forget it
& become enmeshed in another.

WINTER CALENDAR

I want to explain these impressions
                how I can't have one unified thought
& the snow is falling   silent in my childhood.

It happens every day that I let it happen
        like a ship drifting in so much darkness
that it becomes the darkness.

I am healing & it has made me brave
enough to let emotion into my life again

                        & also memory
        & how nothing makes organized sense.
I would stare out the window
in content stasis / there was no hurt for anyone

& I wanted it to last.
I spent a lot of time deluding myself
feeling safe inside a structure
                & only functioning.

I'm better now / I feel everything all at once
        & I can't keep track of anything
but I know all of it is real.
Mostly I don't have any idea
what's happening in my heart.

        It happens fast but then the making sense of it
is slow   or else doesn't happen at all.

RHYTHMIC APPERCEPTION

I lose my coffee mug somewhere in the house
on purpose
so that I have something to do

a reason to wander from room to room

looking at all the books on the shelves
& the walls I didn't paint.
They are a color I didn't agree to

but now live with.
Every window is open at the same time

& I'm not afraid. I flip the pages
of my yellow legal pad to see if there are any phrases
I forgot to use somewhere, to put them in meaningful

context, because accumulation is the only thing I trust.
I smash my face into the glass of your face
until nothing is left of either of us.

Early each morning, the neighbor dog barks
& wakes me up & I wish it would stop.
I'm finding it impossible to imagine anything

other than what is.
My personal life often takes over
& makes it tough to get any work done

or make dinner at a decent hour.

I type a lot of words into a Word document
to make myself feel better

but I'm just transferring impressions
between media
& there's no thought involved

& the dishes are piled in the sink for no good reason.
Later, I'm almost asleep. You begin to barely

touch spots on my back
that I can't predict or look forward to
                    or even remember. You are not me

            but you have let me get so close
that sometimes I forget.

ANOTHER NEW WORLD

Some hearts are smarter than others.
        I keep mine dumb
maybe a little too open to being awful
maybe too close to the darkness
because I worry that a predictable compass
makes the journey a bore
          or else I'm deficient in some other way,
not able to depend on the pleasures
already around me.
I've always been convinced
I could touch an angel if I reached
is something I read in an inspirational book
but it has stayed with me.
I'm exhausted   at the prospect of dealing with
my contradictions or apologizing for the difference
between how I act & what I feel when I sit
like a galaxy in frantic balance with itself.
I reject any desire   to understand
the bulky machine of responsibility
& consequence lodged in my chest. I reckon
the weight of my soul using flawed methods.
        Sometimes I have visions
but if I described them, you'd laugh. No epiphany,
nothing biblical. They're more opulent, like a hotel
with large bathrooms, mirrors everywhere,
& my own face looking back   expectant
like a sweet lost dope. The apparatus inside
is just something I learned from television,
      from a few old records,
& is not real spirit, not actual fire, not your breath
in my ear which I can't stop feeling
even here where everything is still, & so solid.
What you need most can't be found
in this regular world. It's not on your phone
no matter how often you check.

ACTION / INACTION

I try hard not to move.
I don't want to displace anything
          or even choose one thing over something else
because then something gets lost.

I would be responsible
          & would fill with regret.

I saw three people walking down the street
& none of them   none of them   none of them saw me.

I think about two different ways
to drive to the bakery but I just meander instead
          & make it there anyway.
I want to buy a half dozen poppy seed pastries.

Sometimes when I'm just waking up
I put my head against the wall
          & I can feel how big everything is.

I would like to know who will miss me most when I'm dead.
          I need to know because I will call them

so we can both benefit   now when empathy will do us the most good.

All afternoon I drink small glasses of orange juice.
No one understands this   but no one finds fault.

DECOHERENCE
suite // 2

Too much racket in my ears drilling
            past this comfortable head / of private thought
in all this fresh dawn light   & each of these
minutes pass exactly like minutes which means
            unheeded / or mostly spent
                    & unassimilated

& shocking in their number.
            When I took out my black sweater to put on against the chill
                    I unfolded it to find a single curled
                            autumn hair.

It made me stop.
                    Despite all this chaos
I'm trying to write a simple poem
that is so clearly about you / & how even
                            knowing
there is a determinate you / doesn't
            make it   any / easier to connect.

Vexed in this conversation about how / we can't
            trust our memories   or even our perceptions.
Walking the public way / I say to you that we outlive

even the most damaging circumstances
                                          & become
someone new / with no memory of what it was like
            to live a different life while a crowd of trees

                              sits in immense silence.
All objects are accessible through an intercourse of sense
            a memory only in flashes
the way pictures remind you / that we / kept jumping
in leaves with our cheeks red & our smiles
                        & surely
that was happiness in that moment

        though all I remember is the sheer terror
of my waking days / thinking that my life then
                              would be my life forever.

All of what I say equals up
        to my grim reluctance to have faith
in anything other than this minute

because though I know there were / other days
that led up to this one
                            I simply can't feel them.
The sentimental habits of my mind
        driven by some momentary trance
            the casual access to events removed
from me / now / a current happening
        & the weight of that being as every hour

brings palpable experience / present knowledge
        which gets written over the old   hard
            leaving a blank   but such a noticeable blank.

I can wake up in this new version of myself every day
        & happy for the moment I am in while aware
            of those other moments

                    fading / lost / powerful / lacking full color.
I know they happened / but I don't know
anything else anymore.

I am going to mitigate this agitation in my heart
          through action.   I am going / forward
until any tragic moment is expunged

though I firmly believe there is no peace

with the past.   I will live this
forever   these links vanishing / the hours of this life

                    held together even as they
diminish / sublime & comprehensive.

                    Layers
          of new days
fall on top of me. I can't hold even related spots of time
          together / can't feel every self in concert.

                    Distance is so sad.

But still we wake up
                    every day.

No matter / whatever there will come one day
            that is after
                        & in that will we know ourselves.

In your arms through / a Brooklyn night   I start
            listing the things in your room
                        on the windowsill
                                    on the shelves
            to convince myself that this somber human weight
                        is mine.

In morning light we are finally / cleansed of happening
            & recognize   or else we are solely constructed in time
                        & hammered whole by the events around us?

I am full of reactions to events
            I would like to be emptied of.
I keep seeing every new configuration & can't hold it all.

Or is it possible that a simultaneous answer
            is achieved? I can't write this
                        toward answers...

This constant intensification of knowledge
         this present living into waves of light
                 that are too bold / inexplicable / or simply
                      one more produced poem empty of feeling

has left me small & stale today / with my coffee
as the afternoon moves forward anyway. Other months

         I was glad to follow my own commotion
                 & hopeful / for some meaning in the result
but the process just took time & stopped bringing joy.

                                 I am ready
to deny any interest in the end result / because
what I love about today is
                 the way it moves.

We are our pattern / moments & thoughts
                             laid inextricable from perception
all together in a constantly shifting / unpredictable
motion we can't tire of or discern.

And this feels painfully beautiful
whether or not
it will change the world one drop

C. D. Wright   "Lake Echo, Dear"

MESSENGER PARTICLE

Two people driving through the rain.

Two people
occupying similar emotional & physical space.
The car.
She turned the windshield wipers off

to hear that distinct hush.
Each individual instance of rain
smacked the glass becoming
            a discrete dot   & the rush

of the car through time blurs

                                    blurs those moments
connecting them / changing them
so that her eyes aren't her eyes anymore

they're only what you remember of them.
            The only color left is whatever you can't let go.

            You   can't recall what you
really said   at certain times of crisis
& all this inability accrues   the water

            creates a sheen you can't see through
but it's clear there's something you need to be aware of
                  a force which you didn't respect
            & from which you need relief.

LANDSCAPE & FIGURE COMPOSITION

I fill a whole page with ovals
working fast to train my hand

now all I can see are lopsided circles
                hurt but still floating.
This is a precise observational exercise.

Outside the shadows are blue
                    & even the light is blue.

The people I know are very connected.
            They know a lot of things
about other people
as well as about this planet

but they have chosen their beliefs
just as I am trying to choose compassion.

I think too long about writing you a letter
& then don't do it.

My heart is feeling very off center
& the weather doesn't help much
            since it's so hard to see & I'm trying
to rely much more on the evidence of what
is directly in front of me instead of living

in some kind of shelter that I carry with me
that protects me from feeling or knowing
anything directly / I think this

rapid sketching can help me cover a lot of ground
with joyous speed!
But my new happiness comes from patience.

DIFFERENT DEER

When I drive
I keep my eyes unfocused
          alert to the inessential detail
that is everywhere around me

the crystal snowmelt receding

the faces of the other drivers
          beautiful in the glow
          of their dashboard gauges

the fire that stains
                              the western horizon
          as evening takes hold of us all

a deer's crumpled body
like an anchor on the roadside.

I can't forget it.
It means nothing to me

the terrible weight of it
the dim field-colored hair

          bristly   crushed
into the salt-blasted asphalt
          a hardbright   white.
                    Earlier

I stood on the front porch
          & watched   attentively
three deer grazing together
          bounding smoothly

their bodies so light
                    almost empty.

THE DIFFICULT FRUIT

I don't want to spend fifteen minutes wondering
about what to make for dinner
or about time
                        when to start preparing
& how to balance all of the things I may try to do

which gets immediately limited by all the things
I am actually doing.
                        I don't want to worry about
what's happening in this photo on the wall.

I want to remove this photo from the wall
so that it can stop being not a mirror   or else

I can simply turn its dull face to the wall. I will slow down
& drink fresh coffee at any hour of the day & not worry
about how it will keep me up all night.

I will slow down & stop using ampersands
to extend my sentences in an artificial way
that any reader can see through. The substance

grows thin but the fingers keep talking
through huge drifts of snow

which border the driveway. At home
quiet on the kitchen table
is my new painting   *The Difficult Fruit.*
It contains an entire box of memories
            it contains my voice singing
it contains   so many images that are dead
            & are in no way the real things
they hoped they might be.

HAVING CONSISTENT EXPECTATIONS

Sometimes you know the type of story you're in
because the signals add up

                                     & are obvious.
You know how to act.
You feel safe

like when you turn the wheel
& the sun catches you full in the face.
            You don't even look to the right
because you live in a world you have faith in.

But you are never safe.

Sometimes you need music
with words & sometimes the words
get in the way   confuse
the genuine human ache.

You want everything to go away

to not think about what might be

unaccounted for.   I almost made you feel
like something was missing
like everything had turned
to cloud

            harder to track without help
& consistent attention. The things I can't see
haunt my eyes   the light
passing through your shirt

            though I can't remember what you said
& I don't know how to act with my hands.
            Disasters keep happening
when we aren't paying attention

even when we have faith that they won't.

SIMULTANEOUS EVENTS

You have introduced a new narrative into my life
                    a structure / this architecture

& we will see if I am equipped
                    to fulfill this challenge
          if I can be what you're asking me to be
                    or if I am   there already.
Now   this course of action I thought of as fixed

                    disintegrates / is unreadable
          has stopped having immediate bearing on my morning.
                    Elements from yesterday & before
that were dismissed are now shining   important.

There is a new way to see all of this time.

Light gathers slowly in the tree outside my window
          & I believe it is getting later   can feel that flow

but I'm still here imagining new lives.   I can't stop
          now that they've been made possible
by just one smile   by the clatter of photons against my heart.

I am nothing but my own many problems with living
          management / organizational difficulties
                    within the delicate throng / thrum of my soul.

I thought I knew where this was going
          or at least understood / had control over the variables
                    that might cause the course to veer   as when
my morning commute is fixed   but fraught with disparate elements
          that might cause deviation
                              a collision to shut down the lane
                              or getting off the highway two exits early
          just to see the trees rush outside in different patterns.

DECOHERENCE
suite // 3

Woke up /   cold & felt my skin tight
          around the back of my head where
many of the complex permutations
                         of my identity
          spark in ways that / can't track
& all my insecurity lingers in a buzz of pain

& so pull more & more blankets over me
in happy withdrawal before the timed heat
                         burst / kicks on
& signals real morning.

So many of the endings I remember
                         are in winter.

When morning is in me / suddenly
                    this new existence is fitted to existing things
so it is the dawn of being a constituent one
            awake in me & in this / bond of joy in light

& so thanks for showing me this
            suggesting this new process
when the work pressed in & made me
dumb / inelegant   where I am only required to be

            efficient at modes of assessment
                    or in articulation
of rigor / & my recursive strategies for
                    determining the right answer
from among a field of poor choices.

Because I forgot the context
          all these thoughts are swirling / an attempt.

Wednesday morning coffee already in hand
          paperwork to do
                              some of which helps me
               slowly reclaim my life / for which I have no model

or so many models that it's not much help

when I am faced with a standard this / that decision
with a need for immediate action.
                    Sometimes I think of a word

& can only hear its previous usage too loud
in my chronological human ears
          for my own mark to form.

Frost on the grass today for the first time
          this season / & the neighbor cars start
early for warmth in the headlight dark.

Each dull sound   creates an epistemological roar
          beyond my sense of it / distractions
keeping me in the front of my head

          so I can't bury enough down
                    in the silence of all the things

I need to sort out. I can't hear the poem

& your voice on the phone means
          you're too far from me.

Each single moment defines / itself
in new ways that are worth noting
                    & do not decay though I
                        wish they would be gone
could purge myself of them.
These annotations that were / meant in conception
                            to spiral out
        & include it all in their arms

but instead languish in my subjective / incomplete
                memory
so seem instead to have   collapsed in
        making them inaccessible in any purposeful way

            but yet ever present / infused with this
independent life. I have no doubt that

there will come an intense moment of present joy
            or sorrow
        that will find / itself / corrupted by
the unknown workings of my inner reflection

which only sometimes   flares out / to hold a spot of time
                            as it vanishes.

It's a memory kind of sky.
Let me know what I can do with it.

R.E.M.   "Feeling Gravity's Pull"
                                                      (misheard)

COMBINED INPUT SIGNAL

I taught myself to feel sad / about certain things
                                        a particular pair of eyes
                                            winter
                    how I'm not the one talking to you now

& that street I won't drive down / though it takes me longer
                            to get to the regular places I need to go.
If I recall the same event five times in one afternoon
            three instances result in
                    pensive reflection that makes me feel I've gone wrong

two times I feel strong / like I've overcome something
            or done right with the days that I've been given
                        which means my self-doubt is healthy
& like this I've reinforced the synapses that identify parts
of my life as locations for sorrow

                            I don't want to approach
on the many normal days when I am hopeful to remain
                a happy forward moving entity.

In this model of the problem   I see just you
        walking down the street away
        & the hulks of snow-covered cars block my view
        until there is nothing left but the cold & the bright
& the signal exceeds the threshold required
                            to make the moving neuron fire
        so it fires.

TWILIGHT

Already the heat is too much for me
          the reminder of all those days when I thought I was dying.

The windows in the house are open
          the ceiling fan cycling & there's no cross breeze.
These are statements of fact only

I don't try to see too deeply into things.
I keep myself protected from getting too excited
or too destroyed.

The mailman brings four pieces of mail
& each one of them tells me something about myself.

I have never been good at belonging to anything.

Everything anyone says about me could apply
to almost anyone else
                    so I'm careful not to make the mistake
of believing in anything.

I like to jot down instances of empirical data
which my consciousness has perceived
                    & then refer to it as it starts to get dark

as I drink many beers into the night
a few glasses of wine.
                    It gets cooler

& easier to have faith after the sun goes down
lying in bed listening to the trains pulse
after I've closed my eyes.

WATCH THE GROUND DARKEN

All those rain drops
nudging each other the long way down.
          Suddenly their parts are a lake.
My front yard is many shades of green
but I like this green the best.
Mostly I want to ignore the noise
around me but the crow
with his oily body in the front tree
          yelling
makes it hard. I download
four different Spring Soup Recipes!
& wish the person behind the counter
at the coffee shop had told me something
about life, anything. Not even
a secret   just some simple fact.
The flavor of a favorite drink
or about visiting Budapest
on a mission trip in college.
Above the tree line a helicopter circles
& can't put itself down anywhere nor
can it stop moving in the sky
          knocking all the air
out of the way & I don't know
what's happening either.
I stare too long at the cash register
screen as if trying to burn important data
on the surface of my heart. $3.23.
Coffee & croissant. That was then
          this is now.   Is now.
I sit in my living room then move
to the front porch. My house
on a hill. Everything here getting
darker   & darker.

SOLAR COLLAPSE

I've wanted to disappear
for so long it might have already happened,
every last particle of spring snow passing

right through my chest.
I stand in line at the post office
too close to the woman ahead of me

because I'm convinced
I'm already
transparent & hollow

so she won't notice my nose buried
in the curls gathered at her neck.
I want to take the sun with me

when I go
create a global catastrophe,
leave the whole world cold

under ripples of grey, the clouds
pressing their thumbs into every single heart,
flattening every soul.

Darling, the atmosphere
may be important but it's the companion
that matters.

We'll convince each other to go away,
bury ourselves in the hills, in miles of trees
among the lakes cut deep into the ground

& we'll breathe only
the light that's left
after the sun dims & disappears.

NOTHING I HEAR

I can't even decide to go to the farmer's market.
Three glasses of water don't provide clarity,

I still pace around the kitchen.

I can't remember anything about you.
I can't remember anything about you now

that you're gone. I spend an hour watching

cover songs on YouTube, girls lonely in too much makeup,
inside their bedrooms, all the desperate young men

who want to be so alive in any other place.

I want to sound myself right into your heart.
I want to sound myself right into my heart.

I try to sing the chorus of the song.
Everyone wants those words to make us feel

whole, to convince the world they are alive.
To make the past just go away.

But no one is right
& no one is wrong

& we all know everything we need to know
            if only we could believe it.

Sometimes you forget
& sometimes you just pretend you don't know.

THE DIFFICULT FRUIT

The close & consistent noise of cities
is not at all like the snowflakes crowding
the space between branches
which is all I can see through this window.

I don't know why we're not kissing

or how this house forgets us so easily,
why my mouth is so full
of surprises. One of us will have to be
the one who remembers what this street feels like.

Otherwise so much will be lost.

Each person falls apart slowly
& the other person doesn't even know.
The city keeps on looking the same
& feeling so different which is the tragedy
of brick. All these kids just walk

through a sad time without even realizing
they will be something that gets kept
forever. This is how you make a place.
I keep looking up while typing,
realize you're not home yet.
When you recognize something
of yourself in me, or
there is suddenly a connection
retroactive to an experience
we didn't realize we shared,
then this is one of those moments
we remember.

I give the best parts of myself

to the novel I am writing   *The Difficult Fruit*
so that I barely think as an individual—
every decision & insight, every feeling
becomes part of the overall construct
& I lose my own life. This is the end
of everything I ever wanted.

DECOHERENCE
suite // 4

My ambition is to fuse all the perceptible links
            into one whole / fitted.

It is a flaw / my nostalgic love for days
                        rejected / that cannot be recalled.
So begins this process. So begins this need
                                    to apprehend
all that is distant   from me
                        though much of it is / untranslatable
                        into my existing situation

                there are lessons to learn from such forgetfulness.
I can walk the same street I walked a decade before
                        or even last week

        & there's no way to access that track / without
                    also being aware of the saturation of memory
the unreliable bleed of it.
My story is the same as the story every person learns
            that we cannot help but feel affections
                for even our terror

        but also that we cannot ever feel anything again.

So we are left / a powerful drive to shape
some utterance   some bright transcendence

& watch it across / the sky / to settle & hit
                        but each moment
of this is a struggle
                to hear & not speak
                                    & later speak.
This is a falling   into place
                                the dark concepts
moving gradually   an elusive drift.
It is the voice that is speaking   softly some mornings
                        some mornings loud
& me uncontained & talking with it
                or listening.

Regular bird chirp / in the outside air
like a clock / seconds are a song that
                              predicts & predicts
while I walk a circle around the house six times
to distract myself / all this not knowing
I'm restless at 7:15 pm in the lazy stray snowflakes
          which hurry only to hit the ground in a hush.

My head   builds itself
to a critical mass of things undone that need attention
          overwhelmed by the good fortune of people
muffled in quiet terror of what they want
from me / I go inside slowly
                              & try to plan
          how to manage myself in a way
                    that both does

& does not let the world wash me away
into the cold corners of my own brain.
I look to the happiness of being / alone but

ache with all this loneliness / remove
                              hat & boots &
rush to the quiet.

Impossible to have a final word
because each / instance of talk

                    only ever mostly gets it right
& prepares for / the next
                              an activity
without solution / so that there is   never
anything final.
                    All this is provisional.

It gives a voice to something so that
                    there can be more
of the same limitless / endless / you always

reminded me to keep my shoes lined up
          left / right by the door since the rush
                              outside couldn't wait

& I'd grab my coat & step safely
                    into my predetermined / self.

I want to forget   this language / how it works
& doesn't   & so newly throw

          my clumsy understanding
          at the surface of things & at my own thoughts

& be happily dumb-fingered
                    when it comes time to say

what I am doing / what am I doing
          or else just stop.

I am bound by this linearity   the limits
                                        I am inside of

so that the impulse to observe / changes
                              the observed system

so that I might have been happily coherent in the past
                    of having dinner with you
                    when we were smiles   & our skin sparked
                              when brought in contact

& now the myriad possibilities for that moment / collapse
          into reality   I have not even seen your real face in years.
Every previous moment exists in me but those feelings
          are decaying in time

to result in this decoherence   one person
                    whole / but impenetrable

worrying now about how to reference
          this provisional meaning
                    & just give over

to one word for one thing
          & learn to live again new.

I am a machine bent on experiencing
                   this present
            this always present one / all past moments

only real if conceived / again
in the present & consistent engagement
                        of memory.
What I would like to think about

        is that I can't choose what to think about
in the net of all these interruptions

                        choose to follow even
                        the backs of strangers as they pass
                        & walk away   from me
                        under delicate arch of treebranch
                        city street / some other time
                        you walk away for good

that are constantly vying for / redirecting
        my simple human attention.

I am losing my faith

        in the ability of / intentional utterance
                & I am losing my faith
                        in the ability of / gestural utterance.

Someday the snow will return.

Here I am   haunted by previous iterations
          that are no longer / engaged
with any contemporaneous struggle
                    toward knowledge / feeling.

That decoherence is the natural state
               of all elements   since

organization is a lie we tell ourselves.

Yet I love this inefficient / maddening process
          that dictates the flow of my self
               through just that subtle feeling

of assurance / the tender possibility
                    of when the summer grass spread

& meant an opening of the mind & time & possibility
          instead of a countdown.
A wave of memory   informs
               but only notates   a previous state.

I am finding it harder to understand
          how anyone else lives
or what brings about a smile for them
               though possibly it is only getting harder for me
          to accept my limitations with grace   in that

happiness is simple / empathy is difficult

& understanding is complex   & even my own heart
can't follow what led it.

THE FRIEND

for Matt Hart

The friend calls again the phone that never answers
The phone on the shelf registering only attempts
A glimmer within the maw of a neglectful God
It records the many voices   the impulses   the vortex as we know it
The friend speaks again into the void with feeling
Speaks from one static to a different static
The shadows overwhelming & immersive
A flood of impermanence
Of estrangement & loss   the hope of connection
A sound that resonates forever
A breath of doubt that inhabits us all
My architecture affected   my system infected
With palpable worry   the sound of not knowing
Inside the larger noise of not knowing
Which is the traction of love
The matter of companionship the substance of it
        The friend drives to town to mail a letter
Drives late through the town that is sleeping within him
My eyes probing the iterations of this world we create
The friend sees through me   sees what is there to be seen
Morning snow on the leaves
Rime incandescent on the bark / dangerous on the porch steps
Line of cars on the main street to deaden all suspense
        I stare too long at the deer body tangled in median metal
Dusted with flurries
My lasting human reverie covers it
Moments like this are all that I have
An unceasing mindfulness brought about by the winter
Long felt seasons of reflective weather
Of monumental accumulation
        A man in the powder
Tragically made with ice at his core
Fearfully framed   penitent & wailing
The friend went out to build a man
I also built one   am building one   with him / in concert
Or in glad opposition   the friend is always a seductive alternative
We position these figures on a planet too close to the sun
Entities in dialogue with some other attention
Each unfolding desperately in the light

ACKNOWLEDGMENTS

The Decoherence suites which appear here were originally published in different forms, and as individual poems, in the journals *BPM*, *burnt district*, *Destroyer*, *ILK*, *Phoebe*, *smoking glue gun*, *Technoculture*, *Thrush*, *Turntable+Blue Light*, *Undertow* and *Whiskey Island*. Thanks to those editors for their early support of that work.

A few of the poems collected here are from my chapbook *No Memorial* (Thrush Press, 2012), though they have been revised since then. Many thanks to Helen Vitoria for all her insight and encouragement.

Other poems were first published in *Alice Blue*, *American Poetry Review*, *Ampersand Review*, *Banango Street*, *Barrelhouse*, *Cultural Weekly*, *CutBank*, *Dark Sky Magazine*, *NightBlock*, *Offending Adam* and *Superstition Review* and I'm grateful to those editors.

An earlier version of my "Sonnet No. 44," a rewrite of Shakespeare's "Sonnet 44 / If the dull substance of my flesh were thought" appeared in *Sonnets: Translating and Rewriting Shakespeare* (Nightboat Books). Thanks to Paul Legault and Sharmila Cohen for asking me to be part of that endeavor.

Thanks to Kimiko Hahn and David Rivard – for their work and for their support, two terms which, when added together, equal love.

Thanks to 42 Miles Press, especially David Dodd Lee, for tireless and meticulous work bringing this book to life.

Thanks to the dear friends whose ideas and love, whose support and spirit, have bolstered my life and have found their way into my poetry…

…but especially to Holly Amos, Darcie Dennigan, Annie Guthrie, Christopher Rizzo & Nick Sturm for particular insight with the work here…

…& to my brother Matt Hart.

DECOHERENCE is for Jenny Fortin: relentless advocate for coherence, tender and full of love.

Photo: Edgar Praus

Nate Pritts is the author of seven previous books of poetry, including
Post Human (A-Minor Books, 2016) and *The Wonderfull Yeare* (Cooper
Dillon, 2010), and more than a dozen chapbooks including *Life Event*
(Artifact Press) and *Sky Poems* (Greying Ghost Press). His poems, and
writings about poetry, have been published in *American Poetry Review*,
Poets & Writers, *Writers Digest* and many other places. He is also
the Director and Founding Editor of H_NGM_N Books (b. 2001), an
independent publishing house that started as a mimeograph 'zine.
Pritts is Associate Professor at Ashford University. He lives in the
Finger Lakes region of New York State.

natepritts.com